My First Book of

COLOURS

Neeru Vajpai

RED TURTLE
RUPA

I would like to dedicate this book to my mother,
Malti Mohan, who loves teaching children.
She taught till the age of eighty-four and still misses no
opportunity to teach underprivileged children.

Published in Red Turtle by
Rupa Publications India Pvt. Ltd 2017
7/16, Ansari Road, Daryaganj
New Delhi 110002

Sales centres:
Allahabad Bengaluru Chennai
Hyderabad Jaipur Kathmandu
Kolkata Mumbai

Text Copyright © Neeru Vajpai 2017
Illustrations Copyright © Rupa Publications India Pvt. Ltd 2017
Design by - Roy Creation

The views and opinions expressed in this book are the author's own and the facts
are as reported by him/her which have been verified to the extent possible, and the
publishers are not in any way liable for the same.

ISBN: 978-81-291-4478-2

First impression 2017

10 9 8 7 6 5 4 3 2 1

The moral right of the author has been asserted.

Printed at Shree Maitrey Printech Pvt. Ltd, Noida

This book belongs to:

....

....

WHITE

Milk

Cloud

Dove

Snow

White White White

Can you think of one object that is white in colour? Draw it in the space provided.

RED

Apple

Cherry

Letter Box

Fire Engine

Write

Red Red Red Red

An apple is red in colour. Draw one more fruit that is red in colour.

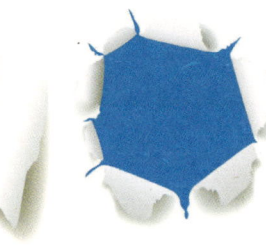

Sky

Sea

Ink

Jeans

Write

Blue Blue Blue Blue

Can you think of one object that is blue in colour? Draw it in the space provided.

Grass

Plant

Peas

Parrot

Write

Green Green Green

Leaves are green and so are the trees. Draw a tree in the given space.

11

YELLOW

Corn

Lemon

Banana

Sun

Yellow Yellow Yellow

Can you think of one object that is yellow in colour? Draw it in the space provided.

Orange

Carrot

Clownfish

Marigold

Write

Orange   Orange

Can you think of one object that is orange in colour? Draw it in the space provided.

Flamingo

Candyfloss

Lips

Nails

Write

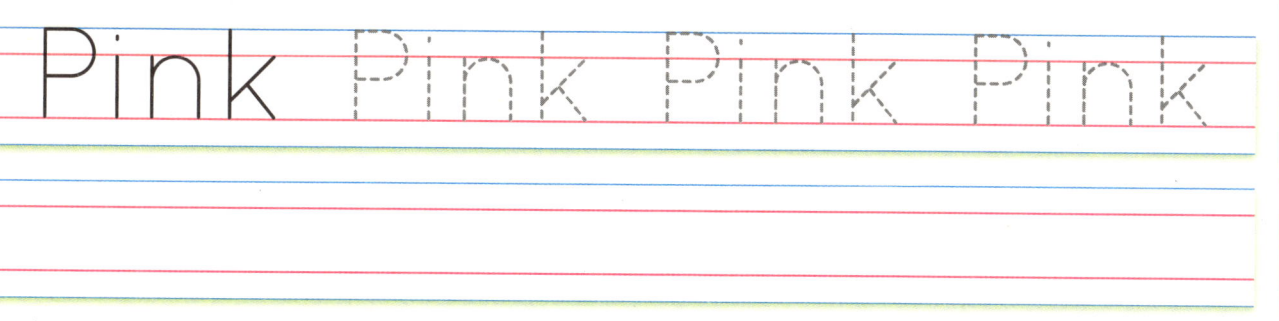

Pink Pink Pink Pink

Your lips are pink and so are your nails. Draw your favourite candy that is pink in colour.

Soil

Wood

Chocolate

Peanut

Write

Brown Brown Brown

Can you think of one object that is brown in colour? Draw it in the space provided.

19

PURPLE

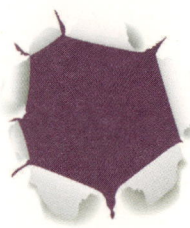

Grapes

Turnips

Plum

Brinjal

20

Can you think of one object that is purple in colour? Draw it in the space provided.

Crow

Gorilla

Top Hat

Coal

Write

Black Black Black

Can you think of one object that is black in colour? Draw it in the space provided.

Red

Yellow

Blue

Green

Brown

Purple

Orange

Pink

Black

White

Colour the things that are red.

Use the colour code to colour the butterfly.

1 red **2** yellow **3** green **4** blue **5** orange

Orange

Green

Brown

White

Yellow

Pink

Use the colour code to colour the picture.

A-red, B-blue, C-black, D-pink, E-orange, F-yellow, G-green, H-brown, I-purple.

29

Colour the picture.

Red, yellow and blue are the three primary colours. By mixing them together we get more colours. Let's find out these new colours.

Blue + red =    Blue + yellow =   Yellow + red =

Draw one object for each new colour.

Which is your favourite colour? Use the given space to draw an object of your favourite colour.